Philosophy
and Writing

First edition for the United States, its territories and dependencies, Canada, Mexico, and Australia, published in 2009

Sharpe Focus
An imprint of M.E. Sharpe, Inc.
80 Business Park Drive
Armonk, NY 10504

www.sharpe-focus.com

Library of Congress Cataloging-in-Publication Data

Whitfield, Susan.
  Philosophy and writing / Susan Whitfield.
    p. cm. -- (Inside ancient China)
  Includes bibliographical references and index.
  ISBN 978-0-7656-8168-3 (alk. paper)
  1. China--Civilization--To 221 B.C.--Juvenile literature. 2. China--Civilization--221 B.C. to 960 A.D.--Juvenile literature. I. Title.

  DS741.65.W56 2008
  181'.11--dc22

                        2008031167

Editorial and design by Amber Books Ltd
Project Editor: James Bennett
Consultant Editor: Susan Whitfield
Copy Editor: Constance Novis
Picture Research: Terry Forshaw, Natascha Spargo
Design: Joe Conneally

Cover Design: Jesse M. Sanchez, M.E. Sharpe, Inc.

Printed in Malaysia

9 8 7 6 5 4 3 2 1

PICTURE CREDITS

All photographs and illustrations courtesy of Shanghai Scientific and Technological Literature Publishing House except for the following:

AKG Images: 22 (Pietro Baguzzi), 60/61 (Erich Lessing), 62/63 (British Library)
Alamy: 8 (China Images), 20 (Classic Stock), 51 (View Stock)
Art Archive: 23, 26 (Bibliothèque Nationale, Paris), 39 (Musée Guimet, Paris/Gianni Dagli Orti), 41 (British Museum), 65 (British Library)
Bridgeman Art Library: 30 (Bibliotheque Nationale, Paris/Archives Charmet) 46 (Oriental Museum, Durham University), 50 (Oriental Museum, Durham University), 55 (Stapleton Collection), 58 (Trustees of the Chester Beatty Library, Dublin), 67 (Bibliotheque des Arts Decoratifs, Paris/Archives Charmet), 69 (Bibliotheque des Arts Decoratifs, Paris/Archives Charmet), 70 (Ashmolean Museum, University of Oxford),
British Museum: 66
Corbis: 12 (Hamid Sardar), 16 (Keren Su), 34 (Kazuyoshi Nomachi), 36/37 (Frank Lukasseck), 43 (Carl & Ann Purcell), 44 (Keren Su)
Mary Evans Picture Library: 24
Getty Images: 53 (China Photos), 54 (Peter Parks/AFP), 64 (Liu Jin/AFP), 72 (China Span RM)
Imagestate: 40 (British Museum/Heritage-Images)
iStockphoto: 74
Photolibrary: 18, 32/33
Werner Forman Archive: 21 (Yang-tzu-shan, Szechwan), 57 (Brian McElney), 75

All artworks courtesy of Laszlo Veres, Beehive Illustration © Amber Books
All maps courtesy of Mark Franklin © Amber Books

ABOUT THE AUTHOR

Dr. Susan Whitfield is Director of the International Dunhuang Project at the British Library, an international collaboration to put the Silk Road online and make its art, history and cultures accessible to all. Her academic background is as a historian of medieval China and the Silk Road. She has written, translated, and edited numerous books and articles on China and the Silk Road for all levels, from schoolchildren to scholars. Her popular history *Life Along the Silk Road* (University of California Press, 2000) is used widely as a course book in American universities.

Contents

Introduction

China is the world's oldest continuous civilization, originating in the plains and valleys of the Yellow and Yangtze rivers more than six thousand years ago. In the third century B.C.E., the separate kingdoms of China were united to form an empire. Over the centuries China was ruled by a series of ruling houses, or families, known as dynasties. The empire was governed by an emperor, who was advised by highly educated scholars and who commanded a strong army. No dynasty lasted for more than a few hundred years and several were founded by invaders, such as the Mongol Yuan Dynasty and the Manchu Qing Dynasty. Successive dynasties expanded Chinese territory, until the empire extended into the northern steppes, the western deserts, and the southern tropics, reaching the extent of the China we know today.

China was not always united. Often the fall of dynasties resulted in long periods where different groups competed for power. Dynasties sometimes overlapped, each controlling a part of China. Throughout all these periods, the rulers retained classical Chinese as the official language, and many dynasties saw great cultural and technological developments. Through ancient trade routes and political missions, Chinese culture reached the rest of Asia, Europe, and Africa. Chinese technologies—including the compass, paper, gunpowder, and printing—had a profound effect on civilization throughout Eurasia. China was, in turn, greatly influenced by its neighbors, resulting in a diverse and complex civilization.

Religion and Writing

In ancient times, more books existed in China than in the rest of the world put together. The Chinese were the inventors of paper and of printing and compiled encyclopaedias many centuries before Europe. All educated Chinese were expected to be able to read and write poetry, history, and literature. The act of writing itself became an art. In the classical period, China had its own period of philosophical creativity, starting with a great thinker named Confucius. There were many schools of thought trying to find answers to how to live and how to rule. Many of their writings survive and remain influential throughout Asia. Fifteen hundred years after Confucius, there was another great period of philosophical debate, and the teaching from this period molded Chinese politics and morality up to the present day. China adopted and adapted the beliefs and practices of its diverse cultures to form a distinctive religion which most people followed. Yet the Chinese also adopted religions from outside China's borders. Some, such as Christianity, Judaism, and Islam, were practiced mainly by foreign communities living in China. But Buddhism, which came from India along trading routes, became the dominant religion in China from the middle of the first millennium C.E.

The Main Dynasties of China

Shang   c. 1600–c. 1050 B.C.E.
Zhou   c. 1050–221 B.C.E.

The Zhou Dynasty can be divided into:
    Western Zhou   1050–771 B.C.E.
    Eastern Zhou   770–221 B.C.E.

The Eastern Zhou Dynasty can also be divided into the following periods:
    Spring and Autumn Period   770–476 B.C.E.
    Warring States Period   475–221 B.C.E.

Qin   221–206 B.C.E.
Han   206 B.C.E.–220 C.E.

From 221 C.E. to 589 C.E., different regions of China were ruled by several different dynasties and emperors in a period of disunity.

Sui   589–618 C.E.
Tang   618–907 C.E.

There was another period of disunity between the Tang and Song dynasties.

Song   960–1279 C.E.
Yuan   1279–1368 C.E.
Ming   1368–1644 C.E.
Qing   1644–1911 C.E.

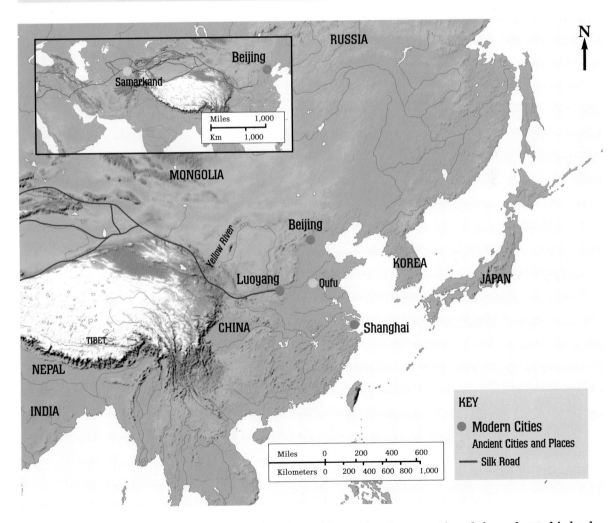

This map shows the major present-day and ancient cities and regions mentioned throughout this book, along with (inset) the Silk Road across Eurasia between China and the Mediterranean Sea.

Chapter One

Early Writing and Religion

The Earliest Writing

In early times China was not a single, united country as it is today but many separate countries with different peoples who had their own languages, beliefs, and customs. One group of people who lived on the banks of the Yellow River formed a large, organized society known as the Shang Dynasty (c. 1600–1050 B.C.E.). The Shang used sophisticated bronze technology, knew how to work jade, and produced silk, all of which were key elements of early Chinese civilization. But perhaps most importantly, they invented a method of writing that eventually developed into the system still used in Chinese to this day.

The Shang left behind a great number of artifacts that tell us about their lives and beliefs. Among them were thousands of animal bones carved with writing, which had been used to tell the future in a ritual known as divination. The Shang "oracle bones," as these are known, are the earliest large source of Chinese writing. Other civilizations had writing earlier than the Chinese, but these civilizations have long disappeared.

The oracle bones were only discovered in 1899 after a Chinese scholar, who was unwell, was given medicine, which was said to be dragon bones. The bones were about to be ground up when the scholar's friend noticed there were inscriptions on them. They discovered that a farmer in central China had sold the bones after he

The earliest written Chinese is found on oracle bones. This is a detail from a rubbing of an oracle bone inscription, written by a diviner, after the king had instructed him to ask a question of the ancestors.

had found them when plowing his field. In the decades following, more than ten thousand similar bones were found, most dating from the thirteenth to the eleventh centuries B.C.E. The inscriptions on the bones provide a very rich source of information about the Shang royal court.

Oracle Bones

Oracle bones were mainly made from the shoulder blades of oxen and the plastron of tortoises (the plastron is the breastbone that protects the underside of the animal). The bones were filed smooth and were sometimes inscribed with details of where they came from. The bones were given to the diviner who held a high position as advisor to the king. During a divination session the king would ask various questions, such as whether it was a good day to go to war. Small pits were chiseled into the bone. The diviner applied a heat source into the pit until the bone cracked and interpreted the shape of the crack as an answer to the question. The Chinese

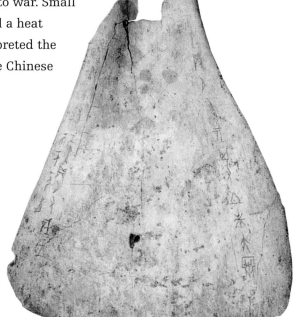

These oracle bones were discovered near the Shang capital in the Yellow River valley and tell us a great deal about ancient Chinese history. Those shown at left are mainly made of the plastron, or breastbone, of a tortoise, but shoulder bones of oxen (above) were also common. The inscription is in ancient Chinese script.

character or word for divination resembles the form of such cracks.

 **Divination**

Often both the question and the answer were later inscribed on the bone. Sometimes the same question was asked several times in different ways but in a form that demanded a yes or no answer. Other questions asked were essentially anything of concern to the Shang royal court, from illness, birth, and death, to warfare and agriculture.

A typical inscription is something like: "on such a date, divination was performed by X regarding a certain topic." The inscription and interpretation was written on the bone using a brush and was later chiseled out. In the classical form of the Chinese language, each character represents a word. More than four thousand characters have been found on the bones.

Early Religion

The questions on the oracle bones were directed at the ancestors of the royal family and especially to the first ancestor from whom the royal family claimed descent. Ancestor worship was fundamental to the religion and beliefs of the Shang people. To them, their ancestors were gods. When people died, the ancient Chinese believed they had an afterlife in heaven, from where they would be able to influence events on earth. The ancient Chinese also thought it was possible to communicate with their dead ancestors through divination and other rituals.

Early Chinese Writing

Like some other writing systems, Chinese characters developed from pictographs. By the Shang Dynasty, the characters were more sophisticated than simple pictographs, which had become stylized. For example, a circle with a dot or line inside symbolized a sun. A moon was a crescent with lines inside. Characters or words were also made up of several of the original pictographs giving a new meaning. A sun and moon together formed the word "bright." Sometimes one of the pictographs was used to indicate the meaning and the other the sound of the word. In Chinese, the word yellow is pronounced *huang*. When this character was combined with the character for "fish" it created the word for a type of fish, a sturgeon, which is called *huang* in Chinese.

For the ancient Chinese, spirits and gods were part of the physical world, but existed in a different realm from humans. A person's soul might leave the body during life, for example when someone was asleep or had fainted, but could be brought back by calling the person's name. Upon death, they believed the soul left the body permanently, and looked after its living descendants and its household.

Everyone worshipped his or her own ancestors in their house and in ancestral family temples. But the people at this time also believed in nature spirits, a belief known as animism. The ancient Chinese believed that each tree, mountain, or river had a spirit, which at times needed to be appeased through offerings. There was also a household god or spirit of the house, known as the stove god.

Ancestor worship, belief in nature spirits or animism, and spirit travels were all part of religious life in many societies and are known broadly as shamanism. The shaman, written as *wu* on the oracle bones, is a man or woman who is believed to be able to communicate with the spirits by going on a journey to the spirit world. The shaman's body will appear to be in a trance while their spirit has left them to travel in a different realm. When the spirit returns to their body they are then believed to be able to give advice to their rulers and others based on

Shamans have existed in societies for thousands of years, from Europe to China. This Mongolian shaman is preparing to travel to the spirit world.

Most people in ancient China believed in local gods and *Feng Shui*. In the first millennium C.E. a story was told in eastern China of a Mr. Shi—or Mr. Stone—who could repel demons. People believed that stones inscribed with his name, such as this, had the same power to repel demons if placed at bridges, road junctions, and other possible places where demons might appear.

The tiger's head was thought to repel demons.

The inscription reads The Stone of Mount Tai which Dares to Resist. *Mr. Stone was thought to have lived on Mount Tai.*

what the spirits have told them. Some people still practice shamanism today, including the Mongolian peoples on China's borders.

In China the role of the shaman was gradually assumed by the sage, or wise man. One such type of wise man was the diviner. He communicated with the spirits through the act of divination rather than by going on a spirit journey. He was the only one able to interpret the spirits' message and therefore held an important role as advisor to the king. However, shamans continued to practice in many parts of what is now China and are also mentioned on the oracle bones and in Chinese records.

Inscriptions on Metal

At the beginning of the first millennium B.C.E. the Shang's western neighbors invaded and conquered them, forming a new dynasty called the Zhou (c. 1050–221 B.C.E.). They also worked with bronze and adopted the same writing system as the Shang. The Zhou did not continue the practice of inscribing oracle bones, but their inscriptions can be found on ceremonial bronze vessels. These inscriptions explained why, when, and for whom the bronze vessel had been made. Some inscriptions are very long and give details of famous battles and other historical events.

Bronze vessels were very expensive to make and only the wealthy could afford them. They were not generally used in everyday life but for rituals, during which the living would pray

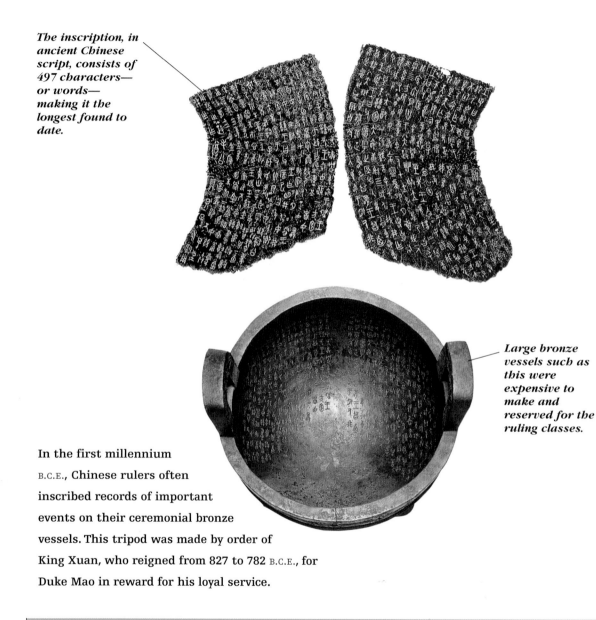

The inscription, in ancient Chinese script, consists of 497 characters— or words— making it the longest found to date.

Large bronze vessels such as this were expensive to make and reserved for the ruling classes.

In the first millennium B.C.E., Chinese rulers often inscribed records of important events on their ceremonial bronze vessels. This tripod was made by order of King Xuan, who reigned from 827 to 782 B.C.E., for Duke Mao in reward for his loyal service.

2000 B.C.E.	1500 B.C.E.	
Xia c. 2100–1600 B.C.E.		Shang c. 1600–1050 B.C.E.
		Oracle bones inscribed

for and make offerings to their ancestors. The king had the largest and most expensive ritual set, which included bowls and jugs for offerings of food and wine. The rituals were an essential part of the religious practices of the Shang and Zhou dynasties. Jade, a very hard stone that took great skill to carve, was the other main material used for ritual implements. The ritual vessels were buried with the ruler and nobles when they died because the Zhou believed the dead could use them in their afterlife. Many ritual implements, preserved in the tombs, have survived through time.

Because of their beliefs, the ancient Chinese buried their dead with the goods and money they would need for their afterlife. As was the custom in Egypt, the servants and attendants of a nobleman were also killed and buried with him. However, this practice faded during the Zhou Dynasty, and models of people were used instead. This was the case with First Emperor Qin (259–210 B.C.E.) who was buried with a complete army made up of terracotta soldiers.

Early Literature

The earliest Chinese writings that have been passed down to us are called the *Yijing, Shujing,* and the *Shijing. Jing* means a classical text, or classic. *Yi* means changes, *shu* means historical documents, and *shi* means poetry. So the translations of these Chinese titles are the Classic of Changes, Classic of History, and the Classic of Poetry. These books and others that have survived from the period have a similar status to the Greek classics of the West. Although their authors are usually unknown or are legendary figures from the distant past, the classics can tell us a great deal about ancient Chinese life and culture.

The Classic of Changes

The Classic of Changes is a manual on divination. By around 1000 B.C.E., the practice of telling the future with oracle bones had died out. Instead, people would perform complex routines of dropping bundles of dried yarrow stalks. The particular patterns formed when six stalks were dropped were represented by 64 symbols called hexagrams, which show every possible combination of six broken and unbroken stalks. The Classic of Changes tells how to interpret the hexagrams to decide which is the best approach or action in a given situation. In ancient times, the Classic of Changes was used not only in divination but also to justify decisions, such as whether to go to war or to predict the demise of a ruler. The Classic of Changes, or *Yijing*, is sometimes referred to as *I Ching.*

		500 B.C.E.	Qin Dynasty 221–206 B.C.E.	1 C.E.
	Zhou c. 1050–221 B.C.E.		Warring States Period	Han Dynasty 206 B.C.E.–220 C.E.
	Duke Mao Tripod inscribed	Classic of Poetry compiled	Earliest chapters of Classic of History compiled	Emperor Qin dies 210 B.C.E.

The Classic of History

Some chapters of the Classic of History date from the fourth century B.C.E. or earlier, but they record events of even earlier peoples, including the Shang and their predecessors, the Xia, who lived from around 2100 to 1600 B.C.E. One of the documents in the Classic of History is a record of a speech to the people made by the founder of the Shang in justifying his decision to attack the Xia:

Be this known to you and heed me all who hear my words: I am no young man looking simply to stir up trouble. The ruler of Xia has done much evil and Heaven has instructed me to put him to death. You have said to me, "You will show no mercy on us but will lay waste our villages as you march to defeat Xia." I hear your words, but the ruler of Xia has done much wrong. I must follow Heaven's instructions.

Discovered in 1974, the tomb complex of the First Emperor Qin contains more than 8,000 lifesize terracotta models of warriors, servants, horses and chariots, all individually finished.

The Classic of Poetry

The three hundred or so poems in the Classic of Poetry were probably brought together about 600 B.C.E., but many of them date from earlier and had been handed down in an oral tradition. Some tell of the early rulers of the Zhou Dynasty (1050–221 B.C.E.) and their military campaigns, but there are also love poems and folk songs. These were sung during various activities, such as picking mulberry leaves for feeding to silkworms. They show that there was a rich oral and musical tradition at this time. Other poems have been interpreted as political criticism, such as a poem about a huge rat that makes life difficult. Some think this refers to a ruler who imposes very high taxes on his people, making their life intolerable. The Classic of Poetry grew in importance when stories spread claiming that the revered Chinese philosopher Confucius had edited the collection.

Songs and Poems from the Classic of Poetry

The Cypress Boat

The cypress boat drifts along,

It drifts along midstream.

The boy with flowing locks of hair

Is the one for me.

I swear I'll have no other until I die.

Oh mother, oh heaven

Have faith in me.

Mulberry-Picking Song

Among ten acres of orchard

Slowly the mulberry pickers go

Shall you and I return together?

Love Tokens

She threw a quince to me

I returned a precious garnet

It was no equal return

But by this our love will last.

Poem of the Giant Rat

Huge rat, huge rat

eat my millet no more.

For three years I've fed you,

Yet you pay me no heed.

I swear that I will leave you

And go to a happier land.

A happy land, a happy land,

And there I will find my place.

Going to War

In the sixth month all was in tumult.

The war chariots were prepared

with their sturdy four stallion teams

Kits and coffins were loaded up.

Chapter Two

The Hundred Schools of Thought

During the Spring and Autumn and Warring States periods (770–221 B.C.E.), many different groups and individuals tried to come up with a solution to the questions of how people ought to live and how rulers should govern. These philosophical thoughts and ideas were developed and discussed freely, leading to an era of great cultural and intellectual development. This period is known today as "The Hundred Schools of Thought." Wise scholars, sometimes accompanied by students, would wander the country offering advice and guidance to state rulers who would employ them in their courts. Many of the different philosophical schools and thinkers left behind writings, but only a few of their names survive. Some remain influential in China and neighboring countries even today.

Confucius: The First Chinese Philosopher

Around 500 B.C.E. a man traveled from his home in what is now eastern China in search of work. He was trying to find a ruler he could respect and who would employ him as an official and moral advisor. This was a time when the country was divided into many states. None of the kings the man had met had lived up to his ideal and he eventually returned home an old man and died a few years later. He did not write down his teachings, yet, more than two and a half thousand years later, this man is still known. He was Confucius (551–479 B.C.E.), the first and most famous Chinese philosopher. We know about him because of his students, who passed on their teacher's words. His sayings survive in a small book called *The Analects of Confucius*.

The Confucian temple in Beijing is also known as the "Altar of the Master Teacher." It dates back to the 1200s, although the original gray roof tiles were replaced by yellow tiles in 1737.

In Chinese, Confucius's name is Kongzi, which means Master (or Professor) Kong. He was born to a poor but noble family in present-day Shandong province in eastern China in a town called Qufu, which was then part of the state of Lu. His father died when he was young. Confucius worked as an official in the state of Lu until he was in his fifties, but was disillusioned by the king, who did not listen to his advice. He traveled from state to state for about thirteen years, taking some of his students with him, but found no one he could respect, and so he returned home.

Confucius had a loyal following of student-disciples. Unlike many of his contemporaries, he did not refuse to teach those who were not from rich backgrounds and noble families. Confucius's main ambition was not as a teacher but as a political advisor. His philosophy concerned ethics and, by extension, politics. He said, *"Government is synonymous with righteousness. If the king is righteous, how could anyone dare to be crooked?"*

Although Confucius did not believe in the ancestral gods that many people worshipped in the Shang Dynasty, he still believed that rituals were an essential part of good government because they helped keep the world in harmony. In fact, harmony became central to Chinese political beliefs. Confucius believed that everything in the world, including heaven and earth, is connected. If there was an earthquake, for example, it was a sign of disharmony, caused perhaps by the ruler not behaving in a righteous or ethical way.

Confucius held up an ancient figure, the Duke of Zhou, as the model of an ideal ruler, and the idea of looking to the past for a model for government became common. Confucius himself suggested that he was saying nothing new but simply passing on the lessons of people before him. He said, *"I transmit. I invent nothing. I trust and love the past."*

No pictures of Confucius were made during his lifetime, so later artists had to imagine how he might have looked.

Historical events were seen as very important, and were studied as a model for politics. Confucius became associated with two historical texts, the Classic of History, which he was said to have edited, and the Spring and Autumn Annals. The latter was a history of Confucius's home state of Lu from 722–479 B.C.E. Together with the Classic of Poetry, Classic of Rites (*Li Ji*), and the Classic of Changes, the books became known as the "Five Classics." They became part of the school curriculum and many people could recite them by heart. Confucius interpreted the Classic of Poetry as having a political and ethical message: *"All*

A Society of Changes

During the time that Confucius lived, China was achieving great technological advances such the discovery of iron. These advances helped to develop plows and other agricultural tools, which increased crop yields. This meant that for the first time, some peasant-farmers were able to become rich and had the time to study and could afford to educate their children. This explains why Confucius was able to teach a wide range of students, not just the rich and noble. At the same time, all groups of society started using surnames that they passed on to their children. It would be more than another 1,500 years before European peasants adopted inherited surnames.

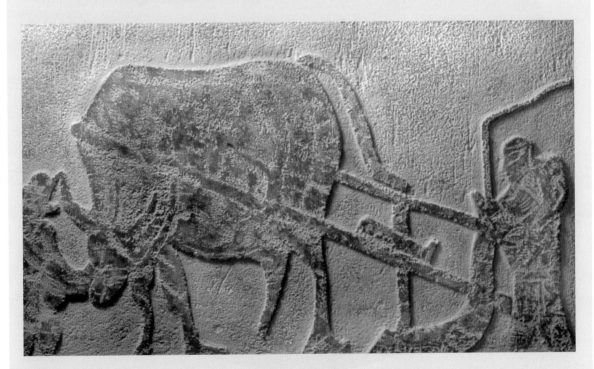

Unlike everyday buildings, which were usually made of wood, tombs were usually built of more durable stone and brick. Tomb walls often showed paintings or carvings of scenes of everyday life. This brick from a Han Dynasty tomb shows peasants using an ox-drawn plough.

three hundred poems can be covered by one sentence; namely 'Think no evil.'" His disciples wrote of him, *"These were the things Confucius talked about—poetry, history, and acting according to the correct rules of behavior."*

Correct behavior was central to Confucian philosophy. He believed that men were alike by nature but that they grow apart. He did not say whether he thought they were born good, bad, or neither. His philosophy was that a man who follows a moral path and obeys all the rules of behavior is a "gentleman." He said, *"The superior man thinks of virtue; the inferior man thinks of possessions."* So the ruler led by moral example. If he acted well then the

Chinese art often showed scenes from the life of Confucius. The back of this mirror depicts the story of Confucius meeting the recluse Rong Qiqi. It is said that Confucius sat down and discussed the meaning of happiness with him for three days.

One of the main teachings of Confucianism was the importance of the family, particularly respect for one's elders. A popular teaching book called the *Classic of Filial Piety* gave examples of respectful behavior, one of which is illustrated here in a fifteenth-century painting accompanying the text.

Quotations from The Analects of Confucius

"At fifteen my mind was set on learning. At thirty my character had been formed. At forty I had no doubts. At fifty I knew the Mandate of Heaven. At sixty I was at ease with everything I heard. At seventy I could follow my heart's desires."

"One should respect the young. How do you know that the next generation will not equal the present one? However, if a man has not made a name for himself by forty or fifty then he no longer deserves to be taken seriously."

"At home, a young man should respect his parents. Outside the home he should respect his elders. He should talk little but honestly, love all people, but associate with the virtuous. Having done all this, if he has energy to spare, then let him study literature."

people of the state would also act well and the world would be in harmony. After his death Confucius's students carried on discussing his ideas. Two students in particular went on to become well-known philosophers.

Mencius

Mencius, called Mengzi in Chinese, meaning Master Meng, was born around 317 B.C.E. and died in 289 B.C.E. He was not a disciple of Confucius himself because he lived a few generations too late to have met him. He was, however, born close to Confucius's hometown and some believe he was a disciple of the grandson of Confucius. Little else is known of Mencius's life. He lived in a period known as the Warring States (475–221 B.C.E.), when the independent kingdoms of China were at war with one another. At one point in his life he went to the court of the kingdom of Qi. He wanted to leave but war broke out with the neighboring state of Yan and he was forced to stay. He probably spent the rest of his life in his home state of Lu.

He lived in a time of turmoil and his philosophy reflects this. He was interested in trying to understand how we would know which ruler had the support of the ancestral gods, known as the Mandate of Heaven, which had been mentioned in the Classic of Poetry and by Confucius. Mencius developed a philosophical view arguing that a ruler only kept this mandate if he acted morally. If he started behaving without morality toward his people then they had the right to revolt against him. If someone succeeded in a revolt to overthrow the current leader that proved the original ruler had lost the Mandate—heaven was no longer supporting him and the harmony of heaven and earth had been upset.

Mencius said, *"The people are of the highest importance. The altars to the gods of earth and grain come next. Last is the ruler. When a ruler endangers the altars to the gods of the earth and grain he should be replaced."*

European missionaries, who lived in China from the sixteenth century, translated many Chinese philosophical works into Latin and made paintings in a mixture of Chinese and European styles, such as this portrait of Mencius.

This was potentially a revolutionary idea because it gave people the right to revolt. In fact, those who opposed the government have used the concept of the Mandate of Heaven to justify their rebellions throughout Chinese history.

Mencius is known best for his views on human nature. One of the chapters in his book is a debate with another philosopher about human nature. Confucius did not say whether man was good or bad at birth, just that everyone was the same. Mencius, however, argued that man was born good. To illustrate this he gives an example of a man who sees a child about to fall down a well. *"He would be moved to compassion, not because he wanted to get into the good graces of the parents, not because he wished to win the praises of his fellow villagers and friends, nor yet because he disliked the cries of the child."* In other words, the man would act out of pure motives that stemmed from his original good nature. In this Mencius was very different from another philosopher in the Confucian tradition, Xunzi.

Xunzi

Xunzi, who lived and worked around 298–238 B.C.E., is also known as Hsun-Tzu, and he lived about fifty years after Mencius. He argued that man was born evil and that his behavior had to be molded by education, rituals, and rules about the correct way to act. In this way, he argued, man could become good. But laws were also needed to control those who were not molded into goodness.

This belief was very popular at the time and was developed further by various thinkers of the time into a new system of philosophy later known as "Legalism." Two of Xunzi's students became important government officials in the state of Qin and put this philosophy into practice. The Qin Dynasty (221–206 B.C.E.) was initially very successful. It conquered all the other states and created a single Chinese empire in 221 B.C.E. under First Emperor Qin (259–210 B.C.E.). But the people who ran the state of Qin were ruthless, and the state

A Quotation from Xunzi

"Man's nature is bad. Therefore the sages of antiquity, knowing that it is evil, disorderly, violent, and undisciplined, established the authority of rulers to govern the people. They clearly stated the ideas of correct behavior and righteousness to transform them. They instituted laws and government regulations to rule them. They made punishments severe to restrain them. All this results in good order. Such is the government of sage kings."

Xunzi

For most of China's history, the First Emperor was reviled for his cruelty. This painting shows his soldiers burying alive Confucian scholars who had dared to criticize him, and burning their books.

	500 B.C.E.	
Spring and Autumn Period 770–476 B.C.E.		
Confucius 551–479 B.C.E. Laozi?		Mozi
Sunzi 544–496 B.C.E.		c.400s–300s B.C.E.

disintegrated after only fifteen years in power. Succeeding historians were very critical of its policies, and so after this the Confucian ideas of Mencius dominated Chinese political thought, although in practice, the state continued to use many legalist ideas.

Mozi

Many of the arguments made by Mencius and Xunzi are directed against the ideas of a philosopher called Mozi (Master Mo), who lived in the fifth to fourth centuries B.C.E., and his school of thought, which is now called "Moism." Mozi was probably as well known in his time as Confucius and Mencius. He argued that men should love all without discrimination, saying, *"There should be no gradations in love."* Mencius and Confucius had argued that love for one's parents and one's ruler is a higher form of love and, although one might extend this love to others, it is not equal in strength. Mozi suggested that the evils of the world, such as war among states and family feuds, arose as a result of a lack of mutual love or regard for one another.

This was not Mozi's only idea. He believed that heaven had an active will that it asserted to influence human affairs. He argued against the view of life that people have no control over what happens, such as whether they are rich or poor, or if they go to war or not. He was also against the extravagant rituals advocated by the Confucians. For example, the Confucians argued that the correct period of mourning for a parent was three years. Mozi argued this was wasteful, and people should only mourn for three months. We know little about him except that Mozi, like Confucius, traveled from state to state offering his advice to rulers. He claimed he would walk for ten days and ten nights if necessary to dissuade a ruler from going to war. Like the other philosophers of the time he also had several hundred student-disciples.

Laozi and Zhuangzi

Two other important philosophers are known from this time, Laozi and Zhuangzi, and their beliefs are now associated with a system of philosophy called "Daoism," though they were not linked together in this way until centuries after their death. According to Chinese tradition Laozi lived during the sixth century B.C.E., making him an older contemporary of Confucius. However, many scholars believe that there was no such person as Laozi but that the ideas ascribed to him belong to several thinkers of the time, now forgotten. Laozi simply means "Old Master." The ideas of this school have survived in a book called the *Daodejing* (Classic of the Way and the Virtue), sometimes also called *Laozi*.

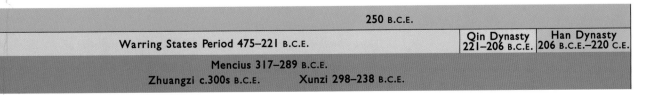

250 B.C.E.		
Warring States Period 475–221 B.C.E.	Qin Dynasty 221–206 B.C.E.	Han Dynasty 206 B.C.E.–220 C.E.
Mencius 317–289 B.C.E.		
Zhuangzi c.300s B.C.E. Xunzi 298–238 B.C.E.		

Zhuangzi was an historical figure who lived in the fourth century B.C.E. and his writings, simply called *Zhuangzi*, are later than the *Laozi*. Although not linked until the second or first centuries B.C.E., the two books have in common a personal philosophy based on following the *Dao* (the Way). In fact all the philosophers of this period discussed this concept. For Confucius it meant the correct way for both individuals and governments to behave. For the Daoists it was a single basic and unifying principle, which governs everything. All these early thinkers also referred to another concept, *de,* meaning virtue. But Laozi's text linked the two concepts. It is concerned with the Way and how it finds expression in *de*, especially through what is called *ziran* (naturalness or spontaneity) and *wuwei* (doing nothing).

Like other Chinese philosophers of the time, Laozi was concerned with how states should be governed, and argued for the principle of doing nothing (*wuwei*) with purpose. He argued that, if one acts in accordance with the Way (*dao*) or naturally (with *ziran*), then there would be no need to enact laws or rules. According to Laozi:

The more taboos in the world, the poorer the people. The more sharp weapons people own, the stupider the state.

The more men have skills, the stranger things become. The more laws are proclaimed, the more thieves there will be.

Zhuangzi was more interested in finding the way for an individual to live a fulfilling life. According to a story, Zhuangzi was on a fishing trip when the king of Chu sent two officials to offer him an important government post. Zhuangzi continued to concentrate on his fishing, and said: *"I hear that in Chu there is a sacred tortoise which has been dead for three thousand years. His Majesty keeps it wrapped up in a box in the shrine of his ancestors. Would this tortoise rather be dead and be honored as preserved bones?*

Here Laozi is depicted on a water buffalo by a painter of the Song dynasty, a period when China was divided and the nonpolitical, reclusive Laozi was admired.

Chinese Logicians

A group of thinkers, often called the logicians, used dialogue to explore concepts and how we apply them. A famous exchange is known as the dialogue on the white horse. It is intended to make the reader think again about the words they use and what they really mean.

"Is it correct to say that a white horse is not a horse?"

"It is."

"Why?"

"Because 'horse' denotes form and 'white' denotes the color. What denotes the color does not denote the form. Therefore we say that a white horse is not a horse..."

"You consider a horse with color as not a horse. Since there is no horse in the world without color, it is correct to say that there is no horse in the world?"

"Of course all horses have color. Therefore there are white horses. If horses had no color there would simply be horses. Where do white horses come in? White is different from horse. A white horse means a horse combined with whiteness. Thus in one sense it is a horse and in another it is a white horse. Therefore we say that a white horse is not a horse."

Or would it rather be alive and dragging its tail in the mud?" The officials responded, *"It would rather be alive and dragging its tail in the mud."* So Zhuangzi said, *"Then away with you and leave me to drag my tail in the mud."*

Zhuangzi discussed the idea that everything in the world and heavens is part of one system—in other words, nature. This includes man, and to live a fulfilled life he should not try to act against nature but accept his part in it. Many people, both in China and elsewhere, have followed Zhuangzi's philosophy, and it continues to be popular today.

The Nature of the World

There was also much discussion at the time about the fundamental nature of the world. Chinese thinkers believed everything was formed of *qi* (energy). The ancient Chinese spoke of the six *qi*: shade, sunshine, wind, rain, dark, and light. An excess of any of these was believed to cause illness in humans and calamities in the world, but their natural changes cause the four seasons. *Qi* can be thought of as energetic fluids in the atmosphere and as the breath and other forces inside the body. Later, the belief in two basic forms of *qi*, *yin* (female, dark) and *yang* (male, light), became dominant. Philosophers believed that a man's birth was the assembling of *qi* and his death was a dispersal of *qi*. Running through the whole world, they believed, was nothing but *qi*.

Philosophers also thought that the world was constantly in a state of change, and such change could be divided into five phases or processes: wood, fire, soil, metal, and water. The idea emerged that the rise and fall of kings and empires was governed by the rise and fall of these

This symbol draws together several strands of Daoist thought. It has yin-yang at its center, surrounded by the eight trigrams.

The Art of War

During the period of turmoil at this time, many thinkers wrote about warfare. The most famous of these is Sunzi (c. 544–496 B.C.E.) who wrote a book called *Bingfa* (The Art of War), one of the oldest manuals on military strategy. It continues to be used as a course book at military academies and as a manual for soldiers in the field even to this day. Most recently businessmen have used it as well. Sunzi took into account the human and the geographical environment in warfare and realized that it was important to be flexible and to be able to change strategy in the middle of a battle because it was not always possible to predict how people would behave.

Despite its title, it does not advocate war. Instead, Sunzi argues that it is best to try to avoid war. An enemy can be defeated by being forced to surrender peacefully or retreat. He wrote, "In the conduct of war it is preferable to defeat a state whole rather than destroy it; to defeat an army whole rather than destroy it; to defeat a division whole rather than destroy it; to defeat a company whole rather than destroy it; to defeat a squad whole rather than destroy it." He also wrote, "To win every battle by fighting before the war is won is not the best solution. To conquer an enemy without resorting to war is better." He added, "The highest form of leadership is to conquer the enemy by strategy. The next is to conquer him by an alliance. The next is to conquer him by battles. The worst is to conquer him by siege warfare."

The text of *The Art of War* **was written on bamboo slips. They would originally have been tied together to form "pages" of text and then rolled for storage. These are a few of the 75,000 slips discovered in 1972 in a Han Dynasty tomb in eastern China.**

five. So, for example, the Zhou Dynasty (c. 1050–221 B.C.E.) reigned by the power of fire and would be conquered by water. Each dynasty was also associated with a color, and the rise of a new dynasty would be marked by certain events. For example:

"Whenever an emperor or king is about to arise, Heaven will display a good omen to the people. In the time of the Yellow Emperor [a mythical ruler], *Heaven showed large earthworms and big ants. The Yellow Emperor said 'The* qi *of earth has conquered.'"*

These were not the only schools of thought, because there were many more philosophers at this time discussing how to live, how to rule, and what made up the world. After the fall of the Qin Dynasty in 206 B.C.E. the succeeding Han Dynasty (206 B.C.E.–220 C.E.) promoted Confucianism and criticized Legalism. Many of the early philosophical writings were lost during this period and the philosophers forgotten. Some schools became merged, such as Laozi and Zhuangzi, and some took on a religious aspect.

Mountains were held to be spiritual places, and many became pilgrimage sites housing Daoist and Buddhist temples. Emei Mountain, in southwest China, is one of the four Buddhist sacred mountains.

Chapter Three

Classical Religions

Shamanistic practices had become part of Chinese religious life by the time of the Han Dynasty (206 B.C.E.–220 C.E.), which defeated the Qin Dynasty in 206 B.C.E. The two philosophers Confucius and Laozi became the focus of new systems of belief, and the boundaries between philosophy and religion became blurred. Heaven, ancestors, and nature spirits were still worshipped, but over time Confucian and Daoist temples were built and people also worshipped Confucius, Laozi, and other Daoist deities.

As new religions emerged or were brought into China, people did not necessarily give up their old beliefs. They continued to worship their ancestors, and leave offerings for the stove god and local nature spirits. But they would also attend other religious ceremonies, such as those held in Confucian and Daoist temples. Confucian and Daoist priests might both be invited to take part in important family ceremonies, such as weddings and funerals. But there were also regular debates and arguments between the supporters of the different religions, especially when they were vying for political support.

Religious Daoism

During the time of the Han Dynasty (206 B.C.E.–220 C.E.) the writings of Laozi and Zhuangzi became linked together and were known as a school called Daoism. Early Daoism was a philosophical rather than a religious system. There was no god, only the first principle, or *Dao* (the Way). Other ideas that had been discussed in China for

This printing house in Derge, Tibet, contains many woodblocks used to print Buddhist sacred texts or sutra on long, thin pieces of paper called *pothi*.

many centuries also became part of this school of thought, such as *qi, yin,* and *yang.* In time Laozi started to be worshipped. Temples were built and Daoism took on a religious form. Over the next few centuries religious Daoism became more complex as it adopted many of the ideas and figures of traditional Chinese mythology.

Two such mythical figures were Huang Di (whose name means Yellow Emperor) and the Queen Mother of the West. The Yellow Emperor was a mythical first ruler who was believed to have made order in the world and who created the way of ruling. The Queen Mother of the West was described in a book written before 200 B.C.E. called *Shanhaijing* (Classic of Mountains and Seas). In this she was a ferocious goddess who lived on a mountain peak west of China. An early king was said to have traveled to this region to meet her. In Daoism she became the goddess of eternal life. She lived with white cranes and red phoenixes—both symbols of immortality—in a golden palace by a lake. She had a peach tree that, every three thousand years, produced fruit that granted immortality. She would invite all the other gods to a banquet to eat the peaches. In Daoist temples Laozi is often shown holding a peach.

Daoists believed that by cultivating their *qi* with breathing exercises and forms of movement, anyone could attain immortality. They believed that the immortals lived on mountainous islands east of China. Even though emperors carried out Confucian rituals, many had a personal belief in immortality. One emperor sent an expedition by sea to try to find these islands of the immortals and another devoted much energy trying to meet them. He built towers and left dried meat and fruit on them because one of his advisors had said, *"I believe the immortals could be induced to come, for they like to live in towers."* By the same reasoning, mountains became places of pilgrimage and temples and Daoist monasteries were often built on their peaks. Tombs were filled with terracotta models of the servants, animals, clothing, and goods needed for the afterlife. Some emperors were buried in suits made of jade pieces (jade was thought to preserve the body), held together by gold and silver thread.

While these ideas were developing in China, another religion came into the land, with its own complex ideas about life and death. This was Buddhism, which had already adapted many ideas from traditional Indian beliefs. In turn, Daoism adopted many

Huang Di, the Yellow Emperor, was a mythical figure in the mists of ancient Chinese legend. Over the centuries, artists have had to imagine how he might have looked.

There are five mountains in China considered important Daoist sites. These mountains represent the five points of the compass and the center. Mount Hua in Shaanxi province is the sacred mountain of the west.

Buddhist ideas and practices, including people becoming monks or nuns and living in monasteries. But other Daoists, instead of becoming monks, chose to become hermits. This was especially the case in the period after the Han Dynasty fell in 220 C.E., when China was again divided. Disillusioned with political life, many of the educated elite withdrew from official life, lived among nature, drank wine, and wrote poetry. This lifestyle change remained an ideal for the Chinese official.

Buddhism Arrives from India

At the end of the second century B.C.E., China started to expand and occupy lands to its west. At the same time, the Roman Empire in Europe learned about Chinese silk, something only the Chinese understood how to produce. A trade began in which silk from China was transported thousands of miles by land and sea to the Roman Empire. Many other goods were also traded, some between empires and kingdoms in between including Africa, Persia, and India. These great trade networks are now known simply as the Silk Road.

Merchants, soldiers, diplomats, and monks all traveled these routes spreading ideas and systems of beliefs from their own countries. By about the first century C.E. the ideas of Buddhism reached China. Over the next few hundred years it became firmly established throughout China and for many centuries after this it was the dominant religion there.

Buddhism had originally risen in ancient India, founded by Siddhartha Gautama. He lived from about 565 to about 485 B.C.E., making him a contemporary of Confucius. As a prince, his home was the royal palace of Kapilavastu (in present-day southern Nepal) and he grew up behind its walls, being raised as a Hindu and marrying a woman with whom he had a son.

Poems by Tao Qian (365–427 C.E.)

Written While Drunk

I built a cottage among the realm of man,
but heard no noise from wagons and horses.
I ask you, how can that be?
When a mind is far away, the world seems remote.
I pluck a chrysanthemum by the eastern fence
and gaze at the distant mountains to the south.
The mountain mist gleams in the twilight,
and the birds fly home in formation.
There is a revelation in this scene,
but I have not the words to tell it.

Returning to the Country

When young I took no comfort in common things
My nature clung to mountains and hills.
But I erred and fell into mundane life
I was entangled for thirteen years. ...
For such a long time I was ensnared
But now I return to the natural way.

Statues and paintings of Buddha in all cultures show a fleshy lump on top of his head, often mistaken for a bun.

The hand gesture shown here—hand held up, palm facing out—is commonly used on sculptures of the Buddha. It tells the viewer not to be afraid.

In the form of Buddhism that became popular in China, Buddha can take many forms, such as that shown in this bronze figurine created in the Sui Dynasty (589–618 C.E.).

Buddha's long earlobes are another distinguishing feature.

The outer robe is covered with designs representing elements of the entire Buddhist universe, including the six different classes of beings: the gods or devas, asuras, humans, animals, ghosts, and hell beings.

Buddha is often shown with monks and *bodhisattvas* in attendance, as in this detail from a tenth-century painting on silk found near Dunhuang. *Bodhisattvas* are beings who have reached the point of enlightenment but chose to stay on earth to help other beings.

He had no way of understanding the suffering of age, illness, and death until he went on visits outside the palace, where he encountered an old man, a sick man, a corpse, and an ascetic (someone who lives by a strict regime of denying themselves any luxury). He decided to leave the palace and spent six years living an ascetic lifestyle based on ancient Indian teachings. He then gave this up for what he called the Middle Way, so starting the Buddhist religion. He gave his first sermon soon after and continued to preach for the next forty-five years. He died at the age of eighty.

Early Buddhism taught that it was necessary to follow the life of a monk to escape the cycle of suffering and to achieve enlightenment. Becoming a monk means giving up the things to which you are attached, such as your family and personal possessions, and dedicating your life to your religion. It is also necessary to transform your mind through study and meditation. Ordinary people could carry out good deeds, such as donating food to monks, and eventually hope to be reborn as monks.

During the first century B.C.E. another school emerged which became very popular and was later to be dominant in China. This school popularized the idea that ordinary people could also attain enlightenment without the need to take up the monastic life. This was especially appealing to the Chinese, who respected the Confucian emphasis on family life.

The Buddhist Underworld

Buddhism had adopted an earlier Indian idea of the six forms of being. People were characterized by the "karmic debt" they had built up in former existences because of any bad deeds they had committed. However, carrying out good deeds would pay off this debt. When there was no debt left, it was believed, there was then no individual left, and this was the moment of *nirvana* (enlightenment). But in the meantime, individuals with a very bad karmic debt might be reborn as the lowest of the six forms: a "hell being." Daoism adopted similar ideas.

A judge, usually depicted in Buddhist or Daoist paintings dressed as a Chinese official, was believed to rule hell. There are many stories telling of the horrors and tortures of hell. One is of a young Buddhist monk, Mulian. When he goes away he leaves money for his mother to give to Buddhist monks, but she keeps the money. When she dies she is punished for this bad act by being reborn as a hungry ghost in hell. Her son goes to find her in heaven but only his father is there. In despair he goes to the underworld, breaks down the door, and descends lower and lower into the worst levels of hell where he eventually finds her. He sends her a bowl of rice, but when she tries to eat, the rice changes into flaming coals. He calls on Buddha for help. Buddha tells him that he must make a great offering of food to an assembly of monks. The monks all pray for Mulian's mother and she is released from her suffering as a hungry ghost. After more offerings and prayers she is finally reborn as a human being.

In this illustrated manuscript of a popular Chinese Buddhist sutra, *The Sutra of the Ten Kings of Hell,* demons are shown herding the dead, imprisoned in traditional Chinese wooden cangues (heavy boards locked around the neck) before a Buddhist judge.

Other Religions from the West

Buddhism was not the only religion that came into China along the Silk Road by land and sea. By the seventh century there were communities of many different religions, each with their own temples, priests, and beliefs. Among these were believers in a prophet called Mani who was born in Babylon, in present-day Iraq, in the third century. He was a dualist, in that he believed there were two forms of nature—the light and the dark. Originally the world was formed entirely of light and had been peaceful. But an attack by the dark resulted in a world that was a mixture of light and dark, and no longer in peace. Humans were formed of light, which comprised the soul, and dark, the body. It was important to live a life that ensured the release of the light particles into heaven so that, eventually, light and dark would again be separate and there would be peace. Priests who followed Mani, known as Manicheans (*Man-ik-AY-uns*), dressed entirely in white and were very strict vegetarians. Mani traveled to India, Iran, and Central Asia to spread his message. On his return home he was imprisoned by the Persian authorities and died, but his followers spread along the Silk Road into China.

There was also a group of Christians called Nestorians who had been driven out of their homeland in the Near East. They believed that Christ existed as two entities, the man Jesus and the divine Son of God. Because of this, other Christians considered them heretics. They fled and formed communities along the Silk Road and into China. Some reached China by sea and between around 650 to 850 C.E. there was a thriving Nestorian community in the ports on the east coast of China.

In the late fifth century Muhammad, the founder of Islam, was born in Mecca (in present-day Saudi Arabia). He was a merchant and married but decided to

This fragment from the Silk Road kingdom of Kocho shows priests of the Manichean religion, dressed in their traditional white gowns and hats.

Although China adapted Buddhist forms of architecture, such as the *stupa*, temples of Buddhism and other foreign religions, such as this mosque in the ancient capital of Chang'an, were usually built in traditional Chinese architectural style.

retreat from life to meditate in a cave. When he was forty he had his first revelation from God. A few years later he started to preach. He saw himself as the final prophet of God, following on in the tradition of Abraham and Jesus, and passing on the final teachings. He died in 632 C.E. but had a large following. Over the next century his followers conquered much of mainland Asia and Europe, and so Islam spread along the Silk Road into China. Some people who live in present-day China, such as the Hui people and the Turkic Uighurs, converted to Islam and continue this faith today. There is an ancient mosque in the old capital of China, Chang'an, though it looks much like a Chinese temple.

Other religious communities that came to China along the Silk Road included Zoroastrians, perhaps the earliest monotheistic religion (a religion that believes there is only one God), and Jews.

Chapter Four

Traditional Myths and Festivals

Festivals punctuate the Chinese year. In traditional times the Chinese used a lunar calendar, calculated on the cycles of the moon, or twenty-eight days. Our modern calendar is a solar calendar (calculated on the cycles of the sun) and its months are longer, between twenty-eight and thirty-one days. A lunar year is shorter than the modern solar year of 365 days. Every few years in ancient China an additional lunar month had to be added to make up the difference.

Many festivals date back more than two thousand years to when most Chinese were farmers. Like the Harvest Festival in the West, Chinese festivals celebrate important times in the farming year. But over time other myths have become associated with them, some coming from Buddhism, such as Mulian rescuing his mother from hell.

Because of the difference in the lunar and solar years, Chinese New Year falls on the second full moon after the winter solstice, sometime in late January or early February of the solar year. It marks the start of spring and the new farming year and is a time for great celebration.

Chinese New Year

In ancient China, as today, before the old year ended it was expected that people would prepare for the new one by cleaning their houses and clearing their debts.

The Dragon Boat Festival has been celebrated for more than two thousand years, and is still an important event today. This photograph shows the carved and painted prow of a modern dragon boat. The deer-style horns are clearly visible.

Most traditional Chinese households would have had pictures of the stove god, such as this, prominently displayed. This woodblock print shows the god as a Chinese official.

There was a "floor-sweeping day" on the twentieth day of the previous month. A few days later the stove god would be sent to make his report to heaven. The family would take down his picture, or a paper dummy used to represent him, which was pasted next to the stove or above the fireplace, and burn it, along with some straw for his horse, some honey to feed him, and a little alcohol to make him tipsy. Burning an image of a god represented sending him off to heaven. In some cases families would leave offerings of toffee or sticky honey cake next to the stove. This ceremony would send the god on his journey, but because he was tipsy and chewing sticky candy or cake, his mouth would stick together and he would not be able to say anything bad about the family when he made his report. On New Year, when he returned, a new picture would be pasted above the stove. Another traditional custom was for families to paste couplets written on red paper on either side of the doorway. These wish the family good luck and good fortune in the year ahead.

After all the preparations were made, houses cleaned, and debts paid, families celebrated New Year's Eve with a meal. It became the tradition to burn green bamboo stems, which exploded in the fire due to the moisture in them expanding. This was believed to drive away evil spirits. After gunpowder was invented, the Chinese continued this tradition using firecrackers, which are still used today. Some people, including Buddhists, abstained from eating meat on this day. The spring festival continued until the fifteenth day of the New Year, and the Lantern Festival marked its end. People lit candles outside their houses to guide spirits home and there was a procession of lanterns.

Qingming

This festival falls fifteen days after the spring equinox, in early April in the solar calendar. It is recorded in very early historical texts as a tribute to a loyal official of the Warring States Period (475–221 B.C.E.). When his master was in exile and was too poor to afford meat, the loyal official is said to have cut off some of his own flesh and cooked it for him. When the master returned home as ruler, the official retired from government life and went to live with his mother. The ruler tried to persuade him to work for him but, like the famous Daoist philosopher Zhuangzi, the former official preferred to live an ordinary life. The ruler eventually set fire to the mountain where the man lived with his mother. He thought they would run out to escape the fire, but they remained in their house and

A Poem for Qingming Day

A drizzling rain falls like tears on Qingming Day;
The mourner's heart is breaking on his way.
Where can an inn be found to drown his sorrows?
A cowherd points to Xinghua village in the distance.

Du Fu (712–770 C.E.)

Firecrackers are still set off during Chinese festivals, especially at New Year, to frighten away evil spirits. This painting shows the emperor and his wives watching his officials set off firecrackers while his children play on the steps of the palace.

were burned to death. To honor them people would eat only cold food on this day and would not light a fire.

Fifth of the Fifth: The Dragon Boat Festival

The Dragon Boat Festival follows a tradition dating back more than two thousand years. It is a raucous celebration. On the fifth day of the fifth month of the lunar year (about mid-June in the solar calendar) teams race along rivers and lakes in specially made long, thin boats with a fierce dragon prow. Some people also throw a special sort of food into the

water, made up of sticky white rice wrapped in a bamboo leaf folded into a small triangular package. More often, however, the food is eaten. The Dragon Boat Festival commemorates the loyalty of an official and poet, Qu Yuan. He lived from sometime in the fourth to third centuries B.C.E. in a kingdom called Chu in the center of China around the Yangtze River during the Warring States Period (475–221 B.C.E.). Chu was a lush and green land of rivers and lakes, where people lived on rice and fish and worshipped river goddesses and spirits of nature. Qu Yuan became an official in the court of the king of Chu but was banished because of a slander by another official.

Like most officials in China through history, Qu Yuan was also a poet. He wrote several poems lamenting his exile, but the most famous, called "Encountering Sorrow," protests against the injustice of his dismissal.

Chinese Dragons

The Chinese dragon is a very different beast from the Western dragon because it is a creature of water rather than fire. Seas, rivers, and lakes in China were thought to have a dragon king living in the depths with his court of attendant dragons, fish, and other creatures. There are many stories about people who visit the court and are helped by the dragon king. But in spring the dragon emerges and ascends to the sky where it breathes water, which falls as rain. The most important dragons, however, live in the sky.

The dragon has the head of a camel, the horns of a deer, eyes of a rabbit, ears of a cow, neck of a snake, belly of a frog, scales of a fish, the claws of a hawk, and paws of a tiger. It has eighty-one ridges along its back, which resemble the ridges of a mountain range. It has whiskers like a cat and a beard, and there is a pearl under its chin.

A dragon with five claws is an emblem of the emperor and figures of this dragon were embroidered onto the emperor's robes and painted on his throne. His first- and second-born sons were also allowed to use the five-clawed dragon. His third and fourth sons could only use a four-clawed dragon, showing their lesser status.

The five-clawed dragon became an imperial motif in China and is often shown on the finest porcelain produced by the imperial kilns.

The Dragon Boat Festival, shown in this painting, is noisy and colorful entertainment, with acrobats balancing on the carved dragon prows of boats, and drummers and musicians inside. Note also the many swimmers among the waves.

Many a heavy sigh I heaved in my despair,
Grieving that I was born in such an unlucky time.
I plucked soft lotus petals to wipe my welling tears
That fell down in streams wetting my coat front.

Qu Yuan finally ended his life by throwing himself into a river. The custom of throwing food into the river started from the idea of feeding the fish so that they would not eat Qu Yuan's body, because in Chinese tradition it was very important to keep your body whole for the afterlife. Parcels of rice were thrown from a long flat boat with a dragon prow. The dragons, as well as drummers on the boats, were also intended to frighten the fish. Qu Yuan became a revered figure in Confucianism because he was seen as an example of the loyal and incorruptible official.

Night of the Sevenths

The next major festival in the Chinese year is on the seventh day of the seventh month, called *Qixi* (Night of the Sevenths). In China odd numbers are thought to be lucky, unlike even numbers, so many festivals, marriages, and other large events are held on odd-numbered days of the month. *Qixi* is a festival associated with love.

Just as the ancient Greeks named groups of stars after mythical figures such as Orion, the Chinese also named stars. But they often named individual stars, instead of entire constellations. For example, there are two bright stars on either side of the Milky Way, Altair and Vega, and these are known in China as the Cowherd and the Weaving Maid.

The story behind these stars tells of a young cowherd on earth who plays the flute so beautifully that the daughter of the King of Heaven drops her weaving and comes down to earth to listen. They fall in love, marry, and have two

---

Poems for Qixi

Pledging our love for each other in secret
On this seventh night of the seventh month,
May we be a pair of lovebirds in the heavens,
May we be entwined tree branches on the earth.

Bai Juyi (772–846 c.e.)

Autumn and silver candlelight cold on a painted screen
Her fan of filmy gauze waves at the darting fireflies
On the heavenly steps the evening light is cool like water
She sits and watches the Cowherd and Weaving Maid

Du Mu (803–852 c.e.)

children. But the king hears of this and is very angry. He orders her back to heaven. The cowherd follows her with their children but just as he is catching up, her mother takes a hairpin and scratches a groove in the sky between the two lovers. This forms a wide river, the Milky Way, and so separates the husband and wife forever. The wife sits and weaves on her side of the river while her husband and children watch her from the opposite bank.

Their love is so strong that the mythical king of the birds, the Phoenix, takes pity on them and calls all the magpies in the world together. Once a year, they fly all the way to heaven and form a bridge over the Milky Way. The lovers can be together again for one night, the seventh of the seventh.

A couple in modern Beijing on the Night of the Sevenths, *Qixi*. They make a wish as they place a floating lantern on the waters of the lake.

Daoism continues to be popular among Chinese people today. In this Ghost Festival ceremony at a Hong Kong temple, a Daoist priest appeases the spirits of the underworld.

The Ghost Festival

The fifteenth day of the seventh month always marked a full moon and was between the summer solstice and the autumn equinox. It was associated with the ripening of crops, but also their decay, and it is seen as the start of autumn. Traditionally farmers would present their first grain to the emperor on this day. He would taste it and then make an offering at the ancestral temple.

Buddhists in China came to see this day as marking the end of their summer retreat and the start of the Buddhist New Year. Daoists also carried out ceremonies on this day. Later this festival became associated with the Buddhist story of Mulian, who goes to rescue his mother

This French nineteenth-century illustration shows a lively scene at the time of the Lantern Festival.

The Woman in the Moon

In China the moon is associated with a woman and a hare. Artistically, the moon is often depicted as a white disk with a hare inside. According to traditional belief, this is a jade hare pounding together the drugs that will bestow immortality. Some think that the hare is really the Princess Chang'e in a different form, but sometimes a toad is shown in the moon, and this is also said to be Chang'e. There are many legends associated with Chang'e, but all tell that she took the elixir of immortality from her husband and fled to the moon to hide.

Chang'e's husband was a famous archer in ancient times. According to Chinese legend, there were originally ten suns, not one. Each took it in turns to circle the Earth, making a ten-day cycle, which was a traditional Chinese "week." But one day all the suns came out at once and everything on earth started to shrivel and die in the heat. The emperor asked the archer to shoot down the suns. He shot them all except for one, and for this he was rewarded with the elixir of immortality, which Chang'e stole. In ancient times the Chinese used a lunar calendar, which measures the months by the cycles of the moon rather than the sun.

In Buddhism the hare is also associated with the moon. In one story he gives his life as a sacrifice so that others would not starve and he is rewarded by being reincarnated on the moon.

Popular stories were often depicted on the backs of bronze mirrors, such as this Tang Dynasty example depicting symbols of the moon. The outer circle shows the animals associated with the points of the compass.

from hell, and it became known as the Ghost Festival. It was a day to honor the dead but also to protect against the spirits and ghosts thought to come out from the underworld at this time. People would make offerings at both Daoist and Buddhist temples for the benefit of their ancestors. Ordinary people would offer paper flowers and other paper offerings, wood and bamboo carvings, and food for the dead. Rich donors would decorate the temple and provide a free vegetarian banquet for all visitors. Sometimes seats would be left empty at family banquets for the dead.

Night of the Bright Moon

The full moon is thought to be at it brightest on the fifteenth day of the eighth lunar month and this is the occasion for another festival, known as the Mid-Autumn Festival. It is traditionally the end of harvest and an important celebration for an agricultural society. This was also a time for families to honor their ancestors. A special food, called a

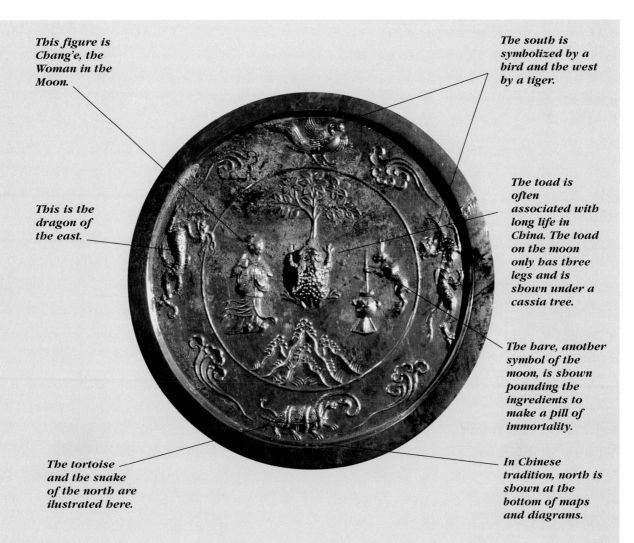

This figure is Chang'e, the Woman in the Moon.

The south is symbolized by a bird and the west by a tiger.

This is the dragon of the east.

The toad is often associated with long life in China. The toad on the moon only has three legs and is shown under a cassia tree.

The hare, another symbol of the moon, is shown pounding the ingredients to make a pill of immortality.

The tortoise and the snake of the north are ilustrated here.

In Chinese tradition, north is shown at the bottom of maps and diagrams.

mooncake, is traditionally eaten on this day. It is round like the full moon and inside the pastry crust is a sweet lotus or bean paste and sometimes the yolk of a salted duck egg. Imprints of the moon are stamped on the cake, along with the Chinese characters for long life and harmony.

Double Ninth

Nine in China is a number associated with *yang* (light, male, heat). The ninth day of the ninth month is therefore potentially in danger of having too much *yang*. To protect against this, and to encourage *yin* (dark, female, cool), people chose to climb a high mountain, drink chrysanthemum wine or tea, or wear dogwood (*Cornus officinalis*) flowers on this day. The chrysanthemum, a typical autumn flower, was commonly used as a tonic in China. Tea is still made from its flowers and the ashes are said to protect from insect infestations and cure illnesses.

茶窗讀易圖

詔忠恕畫

Chapter Five

Books and Literature

China is a land of books. In ancient times it is estimated that there were more books in China than in the rest of the world put together. The Chinese invented paper and printing, both of which enabled them to produce books more easily and in great numbers. But, of course, in ancient China, as in other ancient societies, only a small part of the population was able to read and write.

As we have seen, the earliest Chinese writing is found on oracle bones dating from the second millennium B.C.E. and bronze inscriptions of the late second and first millennia B.C.E. But by around 500 B.C.E. silk, wood, and bamboo were all used to make books.

Silk and Wooden Books

During the Zhou Dynasty (c. 1050–221 B.C.E.) people started to write books but they needed a material on which to write. Paper had not yet been invented, but silk had been produced in China for more than two thousand years, made from the threads that the silkworm produces to spin itself a cocoon. The cocoons are thrown into boiling water and can be unwound to form silk threads, which are woven into a strong fine material. Silk cloth is very porous. If you write on it using ink, the ink soaks into the material and spreads. The silk was therefore prepared for writing by coating it with a layer of a material, such as chalk, to stop the ink from running.

Literary skills have always been valued in China and any educated person was expected to know, often by heart, many of the Chinese literary classics. It was common in Chinese art to depict scholars reading in a peaceful landscape, as in this painting.

Thin strips of wood or bamboo, known as slips, were also cut and joined together with string to form writing panels. The wood and bamboo also had to be treated, because they were too porous to take ink directly without it running. Wood and bamboo were cheap and plentiful but the books made from these materials were heavy and cumbersome. Silk books were light and portable, but the material was too expensive for most people to afford.

Wooden, bamboo, and silk books were often buried with noblemen as part of their goods for the afterlife. In 1973 copies of the *Yijing* and two copies of Laozi's *Daodejing* were found on silk in a tomb that had been sealed in 168 B.C.E. Most silk books have disintegrated over time but many bamboo books have survived, although the threads that joined them together have rotted. In 1993 another tomb was unearthed in the south of present-day China, which contained some 800 bamboo slips, of which 730 are inscribed, containing more than 13,000 Chinese characters. Some of these, around 2,000 characters, match the text of the Laozi. The tomb has been dated to around 300 B.C.E. When they were discovered it was like finding a jigsaw puzzle, because scholars had to try to work out the original order of the slips.

Before the invention of printing, the only way to make multiple copies of a text was copying by hand. Here a group of scribes are copying a scroll of the *Daodejing*, the Daoist text, to present to the emperor.

Papermaking

In the second and first centuries B.C.E. the Chinese started to experiment with making a new type of material. At first, they used old pieces of fabric, boiling them up until they disintegrated. They were then stirred so that the original fibers all mixed together. The pulpy mixture was poured into a rectangular mold. The water drained away, leaving the fibers that meshed together as they dried to form a sheet of rough paper.

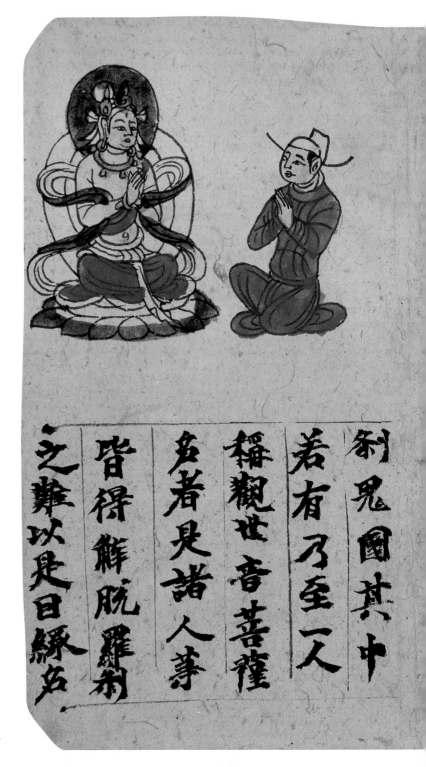

Over time the process was improved and other materials were used. Fibers from plants started to be used instead of old rags. Gradually plants were identified that would produce good paper. Fibrous plants, such as the stalks of hemp and ramie, the outer layers of bamboo, and the bark of some trees, particularly the Amur Cork tree (*Phellodendron amurense*), all produced fine paper. By the third and fourth century C.E. the papermaking process was refined, and the Chinese were producing smooth, fine paper that was ideal for writing on.

Papermaking gradually spread west from China along the Silk Road. The kingdom of Khotan developed its own papermaking

From the ninth and tenth centuries C.E., the Chinese began binding manuscripts into books. This small booklet depicts part of a popular Buddhist sutra.

industry, which survives to this day. By the seventh and eighth centuries Chinese papermakers were found in the Arab-ruled cities of Central Asia, such as Samarkand, but papermaking took several centuries to travel across the Arab Empire and reach Europe.

Books

The first paper books resembled the silk, wooden, and bamboo books of earlier times. Panels of paper were glued together to form a long scroll. The end of the scroll was fixed on a wooden roller. The beginning was wrapped around a thin wooden or bamboo stave to which a silk ribbon was attached. When the paper was wrapped around the roller, the silk ribbon was used to tie it up. The title was written on the outside.

Other forms of books were also found in China. Silk continued to be used for special books, and wood and bamboo slips were used for less important documents and in places where paper was sometimes in short supply, such as in western or southern China. Other forms came in from China's neighbors. In India the pages of books were made from palm leaves, which are long and thin. They were held together with string through a hole in the center and had wooden boards as covers. Tibetan books followed the same format but used paper. This was more flexible and so they made much larger sheets of paper than palm leaves, but still kept the loose-leaf form. Some very precious books were made in the imperial court from materials like jade.

The finest and most expensive books were sometimes written in gold or silver ink on indigo-dyed paper, as in this copy of the Buddhist *Diamond Sutra* from Tibet.

By the ninth and tenth centuries the Chinese started to experiment with different forms of books. They folded a scroll into a concertina to form a book with pages. Soon, they started sewing the paper at the spine so that the book resembled the type of book we are familiar with today. A few centuries later the type of book with pages made of folded paper stitched at the spine had replaced the scroll as the most common form. The paper was very fine and the book cover was made from thicker paper or several sheets stuck together. This type of book can still be bought in China today.

The Invention of Printing

From early times the Chinese had used stone or wooden stamps, or seals, to prove identity or mark documents on paper and clay. With the growth of Buddhism, they started to use small seals to make multiple images of the Buddha. Buddha said that to replicate his image or his words was an act deserving of honor or esteem. Soon this practice developed from stamping many small images of Buddha onto a page to carving a page-sized woodblock containing both text and an image of the Buddha. This probably happened in China by the eighth century C.E., and marked the invention of printing.

The Chinese used a relatively soft wood to make a block the same size as a panel of paper. A scribe would then write a page of text with a brush and ink on a piece of very thin paper. The page was placed face down on the woodblock and a carver would carve out the wood to leave the Chinese characters or words in relief and in mirror image. In other words, the areas which will show as white on the page are cut away. Although this seems extremely complicated, the wood carvers were very skilled and managed to do it quickly. The block was then covered with ink and another piece of blank paper was put on top. It was pressed against the block, and a wide brush was used to make sure it came into contact with the surface. It was then peeled off, leaving the page of characters printed on the paper in black.

There are tens of thousands of Chinese characters, so it was more efficient to use this method rather than carving individual characters. The Chinese experimented with moveable type—where each letter is carved on a separate block and can be reused—but rejected it in favor of single woodblock prints.

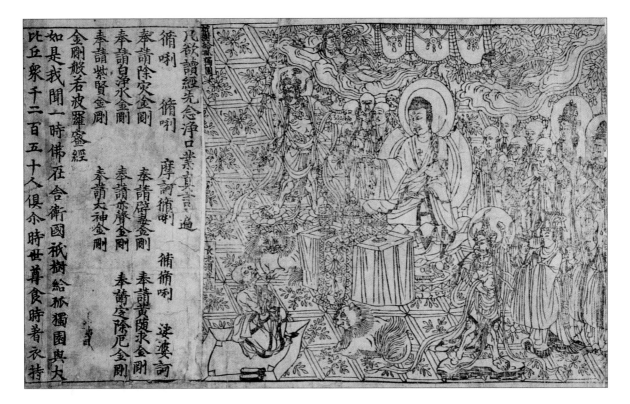

The earliest dated printed book dates from 868 C.E. and is a copy of the *Diamond Sutra*. This detailed illustrated frontispiece depicts Buddha in dialogue with his elderly disciple, Subhuti (bottom left).

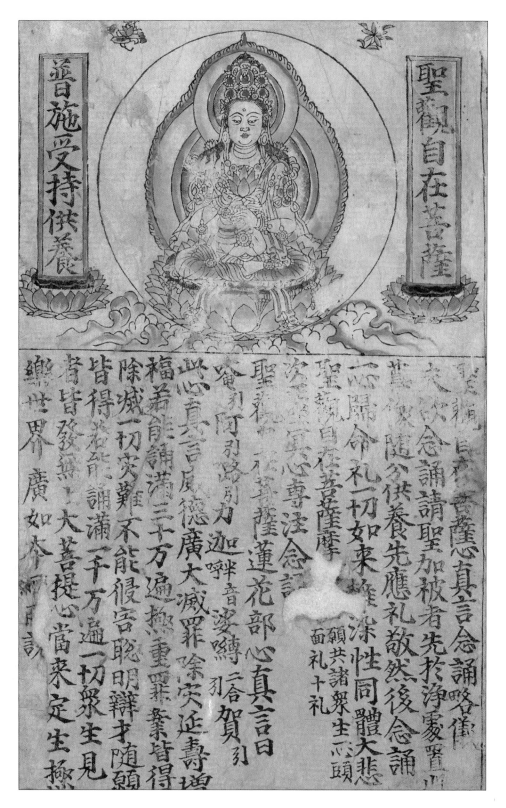

Buddhists realized the value of printing religious texts for ordinary people to read. Prayer sheets such as this would have been produced in multiple copies. This one has been hand-colored after printing.

Scholars would meet to discuss literature, compose poetry, and drink wine, often in beautiful country settings. This fifteenth-century illustrated scroll shows a group of scholars in such a setting.

The Buddhists soon realized the potential of printing, because it would enable them to replicate the words of Buddha far more efficiently than getting scribes and monks to copy manuscripts by hand. The earliest dated printed book in the world is the *Diamond Sutra*, a copy of a Buddhist sacred text dated to 868 C.E. A man called Wang Jie commissioned it on behalf of his parents. There are also many early Buddhist printed prayer sheets dating from about the same time. These show a Buddhist image at the top and a prayer below. They were probably produced in large numbers for sale at Buddhist festivals.

After this time printing developed quickly and was also used by other Asian peoples such as the Tanguts in northwestern China. But it took many centuries to spread across Arab-controlled Eurasia to Europe. The Europeans also lacked the sophisticated papermaking skills of the Chinese and could not print with the same quality using woodblocks. They therefore developed metal printing using movable type. Once printing was developed in China, books spread even faster and became much less expensive, so many more people could afford them. This was also a period when more and more people were learning how to read.

Chinese Literature

Ancient Chinese society greatly valued the written word and it created an enormous amount of literature. Most of it was written by men, but women from wealthier families were also educated and many have left behind their writings. The Chinese placed most of their literature into four different categories: the classics, histories, philosophical works, and anthologies. In addition to these there was also religious literature, such as the Buddhist and Daoist canons, and other books that did not fit into any of these categories.

The Classics and Philosophy

The classics consisted of the texts dating from the Zhou Dynasty (1050–221 B.C.E.), such as the Classic of History, but were added to over time by commentaries on these texts. In fact, the commentaries grew to be far longer than the originals. Every generation of scholars would produce their own commentaries, interpreting the classics for their own time. The classics formed the basis of the school curriculum and some of the most famous commentaries were also studied.

In the twelfth century there was another great period of philosophical activity that arose during a time of political turmoil. The school of thought that came to be dominant was called Neo- or New Confucianism. Followers of this school came up with their own interpretation of Confucius, Mencius, and the classical texts. The most famous of these philosophers was Zhu Xi (1130–1200 C.E.), and he selected what he called "The Four Books" as the basis for scholarly study. They were *The Analects of Confucius*, *Mencius*, and two texts called *Great Learning* and the *Doctrine of the Mean*. The last two were chapters from the Classic of Rites. These four books remained as the core of the Chinese civil service examinations until the early twentieth century.

Histories:
Learning from the Past

Though early Chinese books include historical information, they are anonymous and take the form of annals, or simple listings of events. The first writer in China who can be called a historian was Sima Qian (c. 145–85 B.C.E.). Sima Qian worked for the Han emperor as court historian, a position he inherited from his father. He decided to write a comprehensive history of China from earliest times to the Han. This work, full of observation, biographical details, and true historical information, became known as the *Shiji* or the Records of the Grand Historian, and was regarded as the model for future books of Chinese history.

China's first historian, Sima Qian, is famous not only for his great work but also for his personal sacrifice. After he fell out with the Emperor Wu Di over a failed military campaign, he accepted the punishment of castration rather than the more honorable route of suicide, so that he could finish his writing.

After Sima Qian, every dynasty employed court historians to prepare a comprehensive history of the former dynasty and others to record all the affairs of state for the history of their own dynasty. Without even including Sima Qian's work there are twenty-four dynastic histories of China, each amounting to many volumes. As well as giving details of the events of the empire, they also contained essays on subjects such as China's neighbors and biographies of famous men and women. Most were written following the dynastic model, but in the Song Dynasty (960–1279 C.E.) another group of court-sponsored historians prepared a more general history, like that of Sima Qian. The resulting work, *Zizhi Tongjian* (Comprehensive Mirror to Aid in Government), was completed in 1084 C.E. and comprised almost 300 volumes; it contains about three million Chinese characters. It covers the history of China from the Warring States Period (475–221 B.C.E.) in 403 B.C.E. to the beginning of the Song Dynasty in 960 C.E.

Literature

There were many different genres of literature in China, but poetry remained the dominant form throughout Chinese history. Every educated person was expected to be able to compose poetry and to know hundreds of poems of the past by heart. There were many occasions when a poem was expected. For example, if someone went to visit a friend and he was not there then they might compose a poem regretting having missed him. This is a poem by Wei Yingwu (737–c.792 C.E.) entitled "Going to Visit Censor Wang on My Day Off and Not Finding Him Home."

Nine days without respite,
finally a day of ease
I looked for you, but found you not, and
turned back home in vain.

Painting and calligraphy were often combined, both having equal importance as art. This is a poem praising the beauty of pomegranate and melon vines.

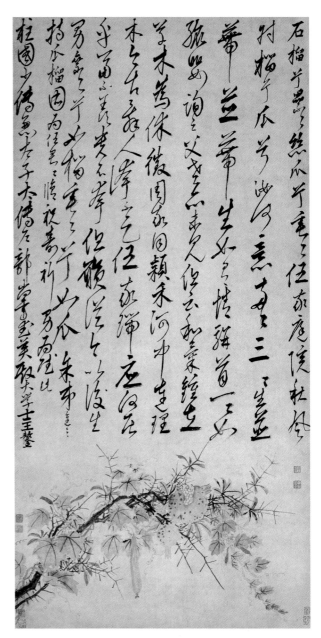

A poem might also be written as an invitation, such as this one by one of China's most famous poets, Bai Juyi, written to his friend Mr Liu:

I have freshly prepared Lukai wine
Warming on a stove of red clay.
Evening is here and the sky is like snow
Can you not drink a cup of wine with me?

Both these poems are in a very regulated form, which became popular during the Tang Dynasty (618–907 C.E.). The second is a form that must contain four lines each of five characters. But the characters on one line must match those in the other lines and the tones of the characters were also fixed.

Drinking is often associated with poetry. Daoist hermits in the third and fourth centuries would often compose poems when they were drunk. The Chinese would arrange drinking parties when one person would compose a line of poetry and the next person would have to compose an appropriate second line following the rules of the type of regulated poem that had been chosen. When someone failed they would have to drink a glass of wine.

Every scholar would have a set of tools for writing in his studio. But these were more than useful objects, they were also works of art. Bamboo stems were elaborately carved by masters to produce brush pots and pens (below) and the finest potters produced small washing bowls. Ink came in cakes or slabs which had to be ground on an inkstone (right) and mixed with water for use.

The brush was made of the hair of an animal—rabbit, deer, and goat hair was commonly used.

The bamboo body of this brush has been intricately carved with patterns of leaves and branches.

Poetry was also used to express many other emotions, such as love, regret, or happiness. There was also a genre of war poetry. But many poems were written for everyday occasions. Poets were expected to know the history of poetry and to be able to make a reference to earlier poets. Sometimes the titles were longer than the poems themselves. For example, an eleventh-century poet called Mei Yaochun wrote one poem, which he entitled, "A Companion Piece to Xie Jingchu's 'Spending the Night in My Wife's Study, Hearing Mice and Being Greatly Troubled.'" Another title of a poem written by Su Shi in 1078 C.E. is: "Some time ago in Chen Hanqing's House in Chang'an I Saw a painting of the Buddha by Wu Daozi. Unfortunately it was in tatters and falling to pieces. When I saw it again over ten years later in Xianyu Zijun's house it had been mounted and restored. It was presented to me by Zijun and I wrote this poem to thank him."

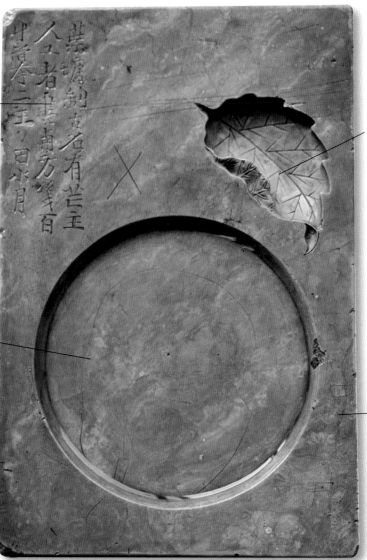

The inscription was written in the Ming Dynasty.

This leaf-shaped hole in the inkstone was for water.

Ink was ground in this wide, shallow hole in the stone.

This inkstone was made from stone from the Tao River in western China in the Song Dynasty. The stone is no longer found today.

The golden age of Chinese poetry occurred during the Tang Dynasty (618–907 C.E.) Almost 50,000 poems survive from this period alone, composed by more than 2,000 poets. There are tens of thousands more poems written in other periods in China. Some are long epics and others are only a few lines. They show the incredible richness and persistence of this genre from the time of the Classic of Poetry dating back three thousand years to the present day.

Essays

Another popular form of writing in China was the essay. This might cover any subject and varied in length, but was often a somewhat short prose work with an informative message. One genre that developed from this was the travel essay, and one of the greatest writers of this genre was an official called Liu Zongyuan who lived in the early ninth century. He was exiled from the capital of China in present-day Chang-an to the tropical south. At that time the people in the south spoke a different language and had very different customs from the ruling Chinese. Feeling lonely, Liu Zongyuan would go on long walks in the countryside and wrote vividly about his experiences.

But essays might also be criticisms or discussion of a certain subject. Liu Zongyuan's friend, Han Yu, wrote a very famous essay, which he sent to the emperor. It concerned criticism of a Buddhist event that took place every few years. A temple outside the capital held relics in the form of pieces of the Buddha's finger bone. These relics would be brought to the capital in a great procession. In their religious fervor and as a sign of their faith, many people would harm themselves. Han Yu asked the emperor to forbid this event. He said that Buddhism was not originally Chinese. This was true but at the time many Chinese people were Buddhist, including Han Yu's friend, Liu Zongyuan. As a result of this memorial, Han Yu was also exiled. He and Liu Zongyuan wrote many letters and poems to each other from their places of exile.

Su Shi was a poet, calligrapher, artist, and statesman. He is commemorated with this modern stone statue in southwestern China, his birthplace.

Li Qingchao

One of China's most famous female poets and writers was Li Qingchao (1081–1141 C.E.). She was born in the same area of China as Confucius and lived during a time when China was in turmoil. She is best known for her poetry. She wrote six volumes, but only a few fragments have survived. However, she also wrote an autobiographical piece. This told of how she and her husband had first met. They were both lovers of books but were very poor. They spent all the money they could save on buying old books at the market and enjoyed sitting together looking at them. Her husband gradually became more successful in his career and they became richer. But he no longer had time to sit with her and look at the books, and was often away.

In 1126 C.E., peoples from the north conquered the capital of China. Their house was burned in the battle. She and her husband fled with their remaining possessions packed into carts. These included many of their books. He died soon after, and Li Qingchao describes how she has to keep fleeing from the invading army and is forced to abandon and sell many of her books. Eventually she is left with only a few volumes, including some of the works of Liu Zongyuan.

From the time I was eighteen until now at the age of fifty-two, a span of more than thirty years, how much calamity, how many gains and losses have I seen.
When there is possession, there must be loss of possession. When there is collection, there must be scattering. This is the constant principle of things. When someone loses a bow, someone else finds a bow. What's so special in that? The reason I have recorded this story from start to finish in such detail is to let it serve as a warning for scholars of later generations.

Many of Li Qingchao's poems are nostalgic for her younger happier life, such as this, which recalls a drunken episode in her youth.

Dream Song
I will always remember that day at dusk, the pavilion by the creek.
So drunk I could not find the way home. My mood changed
And it was late when I turned back in my boat
I strayed deep among the lotuses—
How to get through? How to get through?
And I startled into flight a flock of egrets and gulls.

Plays and Novels

Poetry and essays in China were written in the classical language, but this was not the way many people spoke. Spoken language is known as the vernacular and starting in the twelfth and thirteenth centuries vernacular was used for long narrative tales, plays, and novels, all of which were becoming more widespread and popular. There are more than 1,500 plays from this period written by more than one hundred playwrights.

One of the first novels in China also used the vernacular. *The Outlaws of the Marsh*, first published in the sixteenth century, told the tale of bandits who had rebelled against the government of the time. It is based loosely on a historical figure who lived in the twelfth century and who is mentioned in the Chinese histories of the period. The novel was written in the fourteenth century and is told as a series of adventures.

Philosophy and Writing

From the earliest examples of the Chinese script on oracle bones, through inscriptions on metal and stone, to the invention of paper and printing, the Chinese have always aimed to

Calligraphy is a highly respected art in China. Chinese characters are traditionally written with a brush, the movement of the brush over the paper producing a distinctive style.

Many Chinese temple complexes contain a library of religious and philosophical texts. This is the library at the temple of Guandi in Yuncheng, Shaanxi province, founded in the Sui Dynasty (589–618 C.E.)

capture and preserve their historical, philosophical, and literary culture. China's long and rich tradition in all these fields rivals that of any other civilization, but is often much less well known. However, it is often difficult to appreciate the complexity of Chinese poetry and literature without understanding the tradition on which it was built. A short poem of only four lines might make reference to ten earlier poems, and to philosophical works and ancient historical events. A well-educated China scholar would immediately understand and appreciate all these references.

Chinese culture is also so rich because of China's diversity. Through much of its history it has been ruled by neighboring peoples, and it benefited hugely from contact with cultures from further afield due to its open land and sea routes. China has always adapted ideas and technologies and made them its own, forming a distinctive and diverse culture.

Glossary of Names

Bai Juyi famous poet during the Tang Dynasty

Chang'e goddess of the moon in Chinese philosophy

Confucius Chinese thinker and philosopher whose teachings and beliefs about compassion, loyalty, respect, sincerity, justice, and the ideal behavior of individuals, family, government, and society as a whole form the basis of Confucianism

Huang Di (Yellow Emperor) legendary Chinese emperor and father of traditional Chinese medicine

Laozi philosopher of ancient China and important central figure in Daoism, traditionally thought to have lived in the sixth century B.C.E.

Mani founder of the once widespread religion of Manichaeism in Persia during the third century

Mei Yaochun poet during the Song Dynasty

Mencius Confucian philosopher during the Warring States Period who believed in the innate goodness of all human beings

Mozi philosopher during the Warring States Period whose system of beliefs based on ideas of universal love and care for all humans became known as Moism

Muhammad founder of Islam seen by Muslims as the prophet of Allah, or God

Mulian legendary young Buddhist monk who, in Chinese mythology, travels to the underworld to save his mother

Qu Yuan poet and official during the Warring States Period whose political idealism and patriotism are commemorated in the Dragon Boat Festival

Queen Mother of the West goddess of immortality and ruler of the western paradise in Chinese mythology

Shi Huangdi, First Emperor Qin founder and first ruler of the Qin Dynasty, which unified China for the first time

Siddhartha Gautama spiritual teacher from ancient India and founder of Buddhism

Sima Qian historian, biographer, and court astrologer during the Han Dynasty; considered China's first historian

Su Shi major poet of the Song Dynasty, he was also a writer, painter, calligrapher, and official

Sunzi also known as Sun Tzu; thinker, philosopher, and author of *The Art of War*

Tao Qian one of the most important poets from before the Tang Dynasty, known as the "Poet of the Fields" because of his depiction of rural life

Wei Yingwu poet during the Tang Dynasty

Xunzi Confucian philosopher during the Warring States Period who believed that people could improve their character through education and ritual

Zhang Daoling Daoist hermit during the Han Dynasty

Zhuangzi influential Daoist philosopher from the Warring States Period

Glossary

Ancestor person from whom you are descended, particularly those people in your family who lived before your grandparents

Animism belief that souls, spirits, or gods inhabit natural objects and phenomena such as trees, plants, rivers, and everyday objects

Artifact an object made or shaped by humans, usually for a practical purpose

Calligraphy the art of fine, stylized, or artistic handwriting using a pen, or a brush and ink; considered as important as painting in Chinese culture

Curriculum set of courses of study offered by a school or college

Divination predicting or foretelling future events, especially through omens and signs

Dynasty succession or series of rulers who descend from the same family

Equinox the two times a year when day and night are equal in length

Ethics accepted standards of behavior, human duty, and moral values and obligations, including a set of beliefs and judgments about what is good and bad, and right and wrong

Hemp tall cultivated plant with tough fibers that are used to make rope, paper, canvas, and other textiles

Hermit person who chooses to live alone and in isolation, often for religious reasons

Hexagram (in relation to the *Yijing*, or Classic of Changes) figure or symbol made up of six broken or unbroken lines formed from two trigrams, each in turn made of three broken or unbroken lines

Inscription writing or characters that are engraved, cut, or carved into stone, metal, clay, bone, ceramic or some other hard, lasting surface

Legalism system of philosophy and government that held the law as the supreme authority and that everyone was equal under the law. Laws were written down and made public, and had to be strictly and rigidly followed; anyone breaking the law was severely punished, even in the face of natural justice, mercy, or commonsense

Logician person who practices the science of formal reasoning or logical argument

Oral spoken or passed on through speech rather than the written word

Pictograph drawing or illustrated symbol that represents an object, place, activity, event, or concept, in place of letters or words

Plastron almost-flat breastbone, or underside, of a tortoise or turtle shell that protects the soft abdomen

Qi fundamental flow of energy or vitality found in every living thing

Ramie type of Asian nettle with strong, woody fibers used to make thread, fishing nets, matting, and fabrics

Recluse person who leads a secluded or solitary life away from the rest of the world

Sage deeply respected person, considered to possess wisdom, experience, and judgment

Shamanism religious practice in which a special person known as a shaman acts as a conduit or channel between the human world and the spirit world, and is able to communicate with the unseen world of gods, demons, and ancestor spirits

Solstice either of the two times a year when, due to the earth being tilted on its axis, the longest and shortest days occur

Steppe flat and mostly treeless area of grassland, found in parts of Central Asia, southeastern Europe, and Siberia

Sturgeon species of large bony fish found in rivers, lakes, and along the coastline in parts of Eurasia and North America

Terracotta coarse clay that is fired in a kiln to create ceramic ware that is usually brownish-orange in color and left unglazed

Vernacular common, everyday language used by the people of a region or country, rather than a more formal, literary style

Yang male aspect of the universal energy or life force (*qi*) represented by light, heat, and dryness

Yarrow herb of the genus *Achillea* whose stalks were traditionally used in divination

Yin feminine aspect of the universal energy or life force (*qi*) represented by darkness, coolness, and wetness

Learn More About

Books

Birch, Cyril (editor). *Anthology of Chinese Literature: Volume I: From Early Times to the Fourteenth Century (Anthology of Chinese Literature).* New York: Grove Press, 1994

Birch, Cyril. *Tales from China (Oxford Myths and Legends).* New York: Oxford University Press, 2000

Burgan, Michael. *Confucius: Chinese Philosopher and Teacher (Signature Lives).* Mankato, MN: Compass Point Books, 2008

Freedman, Russell. *Confucius: The Golden Rule.* New York: Arthur A. Levine Books, 2002

Fung, Yu-lan. *A Short History of Chinese Philosophy.* New York: Free Press, 1997

Hoff, Benjamin. *The Tao of Pooh.* New York: Penguin Books, 1983

Lao Tsu (trans: Feng, Gia-Fu & English, Jane) *Tao Te Ching, 25th-Anniversary Edition.* New York: Vintage Books, 1997

Roberts, Moss. *Chinese Fairy Tales and Fantasies (Pantheon Fairy Tale and Folklore Library).* New York: Pantheon Books, 1980

Shu, Shin Lu & Zhou, Kate. *The People of China: The History and Culture of China.* Broomall, PA: Mason Crest Publishers, 2005

Wilkinson, Philip. *Buddhism (Eyewitness Books).* New York: Dorling Kindersley, 2003

Wu Ch'eng-en (Trans: Waley, Arthur). *Monkey: Folk Novel of China.* New York: Grove Press, 1994

Web Sites

Art Institute of Chicago—Taoism
www.artic.edu/taoism/menu.php

Association Francaise des Professeurs de Chinois—Chinese Philosophical Texts in English
www.afpc.asso.fr/wengu/wg/wengu.php?l=bienvenue

British Museum—Early Imperial China
www.earlyimperialchina.co.uk

China Page—Chinese Poetry
www.chinapage.com/poetry9.html

Chinaknowledge—Chinese Culture
www.chinaknowledge.de/index.html

Chinese Philosophy
www.chinesephilosophy.net/

Mr Donn—Buddhism
http://ancienthistory.mrdonn.org/Buddhism.html

Stanford Encyclopedia of Philosophy—Confucius
http://plato.stanford.edu/entries/confucius/

University of Maryland—Philosophy
www-chaos.umd.edu/history/ancient2.html

Visionaivity—Philosophy 4 Children
http://home12.inet.tele.dk/fil/

Washington State University—Chinese History
www.wsu.edu/~dee/TEXT/anchina.rtf

Index

Page numbers in *italics* refer to images and captions